# MONARCH

# MONARCH

A Poetry Collection

*by*

ALEXANDRA VINCENT

*MONARCH* © 2022 Alexandra Vincent.

All rights reserved. This book or any portion thereof may not be reproduced or used in any manner whatsoever without the express written permission of the publisher except for the use of brief quotations in a book review. For information, please contact the publisher.

ISBN: 979-8-218-01695-1 (paperback), 979-8-218-01696-8 (ebook)

Book design & layout by Rachel Clift. rcliftpoetry.com

First printing edition, 2022.

Alexandra Vincent
www.yourliveology.com
@alexandra.j.vincent

# CONTENTS

### BODY

*The Farm* ........................................... 6
*Prayer Wall* ........................................ 7
*Fearing Evergreen* ............................... 21
*Dancing in the Fire* ............................. 28
*Ankle Deep* ....................................... 29

### MIND

*Daydreamer* ....................................... 38
*Lonely Wanderer* ................................ 40
*Anxiety* ............................................. 42
*Plagued by the Mind* ........................... 51
*A Peace of Some Kind* ......................... 52

### SOUL

*Grass So Overgrown* ............................ 67
*A Journey to Bestow* ........................... 68
*Not Much of a Rarity* .......................... 76
*Monarch* ........................................... 84

# INTRODUCTION

I see poetry as a pure art for written words. A beautiful thing about poetry is not necessarily the piece itself, but the meanings the reader will take with them. I admire the depth we can reach, not only as the writer but as the reader, too.

The inspiration for my work initially came from growing up with insecurities and feeling like the follower or the underdog. As I began working on my book, I realized my writings were hitting a bit deeper and were seeping with vulnerability. From the essence of loss and feeling out of place to feeling taken advantage of; to fighting the despair and working for the hope of a better tomorrow.

Leaving my words up to your interpretation is, ultimately, why I am sharing my collection. The picture I paint with my words will be vastly different for each person. And that's the true beauty of poetry.

# BODY

*Part One*

## MONARCH

We came here as shadowlight
with no spoken words
no wrong, no right
a silent cry
engulfed the night
a new baby's birth
my soul to be unearthed.

I remember laughing so easily
the constant giggles swirling in my belly
that cheeky smile on my face.

My eyes shined true
from the warmth of my heart
and the light of my soul.

Not the cute girl on the playground
Head down, I walk around
*I'm not pretty*
enough to prance around in flower crowns
to curl my hair or wear long gowns
you see my body is too heavy
I hear their mocking sounds
*she's so round*
so, I sit alone on the playground.

She wasn't sure how to fit in
but she knew for sure she wanted to be there
and that's what mattered.

MONARCH

Floating on the water
summer sun on my skin
while holding tight to the edge
with my small little chin.

Overlooked I could be
I was too scared to jump in
too scared to let go
I don't want to swim.

I'm scared I'll sink
to the bottom I'll go
drowning out of sight
no one will ever know.

*The Farm*

At the Farm
where the world is so very sweet.

Golden grass in the white windowpane
the shining summer sun
I could chase for days
hop skip down the walk one foot at a time
soft breeze on my skin
this place is all mine.

At the Farm
where I feel complete.

My initials etched in the cement stones
I trace with a stick
right above my little toes
my favorite sight next to the sycamore tree
the springing purple lilacs that dance around me

At the Farm
my hidden gem just for me.

*Prayer Wall*

Just a child at church camp
with a post-it in my hand
my prayer to God
will it reach the promised land?

My words scribbled small
I fold up the paper
place it in the brick wall
for the eyes of my creator.

Make the hurting stop
If you, God, are real
just strip it all away
I'll make you a deal.

I'll serve you forever
please grant me this
till my last living day
be it my only wish.

As I pray to the sky
I wonder how far the clouds have traveled
they come and they go
never staying for long.

I want to be a cloud
to be free to fly
but I think I'm a star
stagnant in the night sky.

My sparkle too dull
for an eye to ever find.

## MONARCH

The long road of a small town
it's not easy to get lost here
every path leads back to the center
the towering walls built from the ground up
keeping me "safe" inside
spiraling around on my tippy toes
I see nothing
I climb and climb
but still, I see nothing.

The want
the need
the desire
to be the Monarch
drifting effortlessly
to be seen by all
the beauty
the grace
the elegant taste.

MONARCH

The swirl of the kaleidoscope
and all their colors
enveloped me finally
in the bounty of beauty and belonging
I squeezed into place to follow the swarm.

The rapped flutter encased my heart
moving me in the chase to keep up
giddy to the bone
but to prideful to show
quick and steady
I followed the ramble rose to rose.

MONARCH

She couldn't foresee
a trouble in flight
with only good intentions
she cast the bad out of sight
a good-natured soul could surlily unfold
the kindness at heart
a mere stranger could hold.

*She had a gift for finding good in the pit of evil.*

All these secrets we can't say
left me full of so much shame
It may never go away
so, I'll take it to the grave.

Buried by their charm
my gates were left open
we were thick as thieves
Oh, but now I have been chosen.

To smite the lamb
the snakes weaved in my ivy
striking the soles of my feet
my dear spirits
they drowned in their greed.

My garden now destroyed
and blush petals weep
the snakes arose sly with my secrets
leaving nothing to keep.

MONARCH

Not a right-minded soul
could help her believe
her efforts were gold
but her heart was deceived.

I was bent at my stem
In wait to rise again
my eyes downcast
and I could not see past
the rich soils of the earth.

But still I stood with great anticipation
for the light to hit my face
and the rain I would taste
hope of a new beginning.

## MONARCH

A foreign feeling, gnawing at my bones
like ice, so bitter cold
darkness lingers over me
my heart stands alone.

*She held great fear of her image being tainted.*
*The darkness wanted to swim with her vibrant colors.*

*Fearing Evergreen*

Just seventeen
I'm embarrassed to be seen
only my eyes see
the deep marks of evergreen.

These thoughts run heavy
maybe even deadly
my heart is empty, and I pity
my own faulted envy.

What longs to be freed
thoughts
may they be cleaned
feelings
may they be redeemed
greens
may they be unseen.

*Holding back from fear of the foreseeable revoke.
Trust and acceptance be my only hope.*

# MONARCH

*She fought with the reflection never being herself.*

I walked around in muted grays
slick white sneaks
and black thick frames
modest I may seem
but my true self I was not.

# MONARCH

*Under my aloof facade,
lives a bright soul with beating color.*

How could they want me?
when there is no me
just a 'she' that walks around
muted to please

No name to have
but an art to appease
an empty face
that nods and agrees.

## MONARCH

I was a lost moth with no flame
searching for the light
but near fading away in the grays
unable to land among the yin or the yang's
settled I was in the land of white noise
tucked between silence
and a fierce, resonant voice.

*Dancing in the Fire*

She makes her own fire
to send up a sign with smoke clouds
she was left abandoned
she calls out, desperate for help.

Dancing around the fire
she'll make it a show
but still, no one comes
nobody even knows.

Anguish it will be
to sit one with the fire
at the pit of insanity
for all have denied her.

The flames destroy her
like water to a web
filling the empty pockets
but she has no need to dread

Because the wrath of her blaze
melts away her pain
dancing in the fire, she needs no rain.

The light in herself will lead the way.

*Ankle Deep*

I find security in the shoreline
where the sea meets the sand
I linger in the waters
with my treasures in my hand.

At only ankle deep
my feet can't leave the land
I listen to my thoughts
as the water rushes over sand.

The waves hold no boundaries
crashing through me
a life's venture
I hoped I would never see.

Feeling broken
shipwrecked on my knees
I walk the shores for hours
to heal my hearts unease.

Holding on to the tides
for my dear life
no matter how tight I grip and pull
they come and they go
just as they mold my body perfectly
they leave me just as quick.

MONARCH

I feel like I'm just getting by
when my lips brush the waterline
I know I'll survive
just a little longer
till the waves hit high tide
and I get pulled under
again.

# MIND

*Part Two*

MONARCH

Those sugar sweet days feel so long ago
that I sometimes wonder if I lived them.
Maybe it was all but a dream.

I pray for myself to stay awake
but all I can really wish for
Is a life
full of slumber.

MONARCH

My sweet escape
my sleepful haze
where I fall into slumber
far away from the world
engulfed in a better life
my eyes squeezed tight
locked in a dream, I am
cherished by the mind.

*Daydreamer*

Sometimes I forget I'm really in this world
my mind takes me to far-out places
where I've never been before.

I'll be stuck in a trance
of a past circumstance
or creating a fantasy
I may never live.

The gears turning in my head
oh, I love to play pretend
but soon I'll be due to wake again.

## MONARCH

So many words I'm ready to share
yet through no fault but my own
nobody is here
my blood ran a bit cold
and my day's got dark
I pushed all my treasures away
to protect my fragile heart.

*Lonely Wanderer*

So many lonely people out here.
Yet we keep our heads down
weaving through the silent crowd
We couldn't dare reach out.
A conversation so mundane
and a minute at the most
could cut the loneliness
that is so steady in its growth.
The impending doom of isolation
could come to a halt.
Then maybe the lonely will fade
among the waves of people
coming and going.

# MONARCH

They say no rain, no flowers
but if only they knew
she's a castaway
left to the desert's drought
she hasn't any rain
not even a cloud.

*ANXIETY*

Yes, I'm scared of the dark
switching lanes in my car
telling stories to my friends
just to get to the end
they didn't hear me
tell it again.

Seeing ghosts in my dreams
oh, the haunting memories
getting stuck in the middle
I must crawl out under the table.

Choking on my food
in front of all of you
forgetting what to say
so, I must run away.

My mind lost to anxiety
I say sorry way too much
the truth is I can't help it
I fell so far, I'm out of touch.

## MONARCH

I fear the river
I know when I step foot into the waters
I may never stand still again
I'll be swallowed whole
and wrapped up tight
moved with the force of the rocking waters.

I'll go for miles
trying to grip the banks
exhausting my body
I'll let the water pass my lips
but finally, pulling my only anchor
falling into the abyss.

The overwhelming ache
that swirls in my chest
jumping from my stomach
to the hairs on my neck.

The sharpest prick
settled in my throat
calling my tears
from the words I provoked.

The work
to build a bridge and get over it
the toils and snares
snapping at my feet
my mind filling with defeat
the burning, the longing
bring me to relief-
*please*

This chapter right now feels utterly empty. Just pages and pages of sporadic one- or two-word sentences. At the same time my mind feels so full. From reminiscing on old chapters and feeling the weight of past mistakes. To sneaking peeks of what I desire to come in my future. It all but leaves my heart lacking any true warmth. I need to be present. I want my days spent truly living. So I can fill all these blank pages that are piling up. So I can feel okay with where I was, where I am, and where I'm going.

# MONARCH

Learning to live for myself not others
you, we, me...no I
I live to be discovered
my mouth bleeds lies
truth must be uncovered
my soul aches inside
she knows no other
I

In the loneliest hours
I grew the most
with a sad heart
I pried open the heaviest door
I stood still in the threshold
beckoning for the stranger on the other side...
"Come forward...let us be friends."

There we stood together, finally
two strangers molded the same
just myself and I
woven as one.

MONARCH

Just holding back something
I've been dying to say
I know nothing else
I've always been this way
I must bite my tongue
but I hope and pray
that maybe one day
I'll have the courage to say...

I don't want to reach the end
and think...
*I have so much left to say.*

*Plagued by the Mind*

The essence of peace will be plagued by the mind.
The possibility that one day you could have peace of some kind.
The inner peace you've begged for all your lifetime.
The journey you imagined could change at any time.

The people you hope to have forever you'll surely outlive.
The built expectations no one will ever give.
The outlandish situations your ego can't forgive.
The broken-hearted moments you must relive.

The unfocused picture in your head shown again and again.
Only at the end will the game make sense.
Once we've collected all the pieces.
Then will our soul transcend.

*A Peace of Some Kind*

I dropped behind a tree
lost in the forest I was
darkness etched around me
I prayed for light because

A sight that brings me comfort
is the sun surpassing the trees
trailing down the road
beams of light lay so serene.

They dance in the street
such a soft golden glow
And deep within me
a warm feeling grows.

A peace of some kind
nestled in my mind
for the light has found me
at the tree I dropped behind.

# SOUL

*Part Three*

MONARCH

*Trust in the transformation.*

*The sky changed colors when a new day began,
and yesterday's sorrows were put to an end.*

## MONARCH

With the shifting clouds
and ever-changing colors
we never see the same sky twice.

The light touches all of us
no matter how deep we are in the shadows
the heat dips and dives
till it reaches the farthest corners
like flames of a fire
dancing on our skin
bringing our body to the light again.

MONARCH

Laying in the grass
just the weeds and me
total strangers brushed in the wind
intertwined now
like two old friends.

There she was
sitting still with the land
rooted in the grass
a dead winter's plant
her colors drained
hallow face sleeping
arms red-stained
her whole world was weeping.

MONARCH

Let it rain on me
take the pain from me
let it soak my skin
get me clean again
let it rain on me.

As the raindrops tumble down
I look around and wonder
are they afraid to fall as well?

*Believing in myself wasn't what I needed after all.
Not giving up on myself was the mastery to hold.*

We are not perfection
we are the wilted roses left in the vase
the falling leaves the wind will chase
we are the heavy drought
no summer rains
a new year's night
with no champagne.

## *Grass So Overgrown*

We all walk a different path
some cobblestone
or on paths of grass, so overgrown
but we act as if
we walk along the same road.

Every rock lies different
each fork sways along uncharted grass
grass that only grows among our own fields.

We have different stops along the way
Some so unpleasant, or extraordinarily great
we hit a dead end
but with some faith, we find our way
again.

*A Journey to Bestow*

But which way do I go?
all my paths lay crossed
no map in hand
I yell to the sky I'm surely lost.

I never knew where I was going
or whom I would come to meet
my venture in disguise
but my mind lay in defeat.

Adventure, I never grew to know
just winding roads
with nowhere to go
I never understood the journey
and the way it would bestow.

# MONARCH

*Home is not destined to be where we came from.*
*It's where we are going, that is home.*

It may never be crystal clear.
Maybe learning to tread the murky waters
is the best we can do.

MONARCH

Somethings are much too deep
too complex even
to form the words
to give the meanings
surpassing the surface level
digging and digging
finding the way
to share in the experience.

I often get lost
between every word
searching for the bigger meaning
analyzing my thoughts
the symbols and metaphors, so deeply.

## MONARCH

The reality is we can blossom in the dark
Truthfully...
that's what happens for most of us.

And that's okay.

Sometimes we got left out
always got lost in the crowd
just a nameless face they forgot about
a story perfectly written
but never read aloud
the hummingbird in the wind
that never made a sound.

## MONARCH

I don't need to stand on my toes to be seen.
I can speak softly and be heard.
Present.
To linger, to observe.
Patience.
The willingness of a virtue.

*Not Much of a Rarity*

I'm a laugher
I walk around with that cheeky smile
constantly suppressing my giggles
biting my lip
hoping to keep them in.

I can't.
chuckling I go
giving them away freely
not too special
not too rare
but free to all
my laugh I can share.

You must remember these days
with few and far between
that genuine glee you feel oozing
from head to feet.

The small dose of empowerment
when you accomplish the greatest of things
give yourself a gold star
or a pat on your back
some way to remember
your happiness will be back.

If tomorrow never comes
I must tell this to everyone
you are loved by at least one
the hate has never won.

Embrace your body and your mind
you are doing just fine
every person of humankind
you are all on my mind.

## MONARCH

Love is constant.
Love is still.
Love is never changing.
Love will prevail.

It's the alchemy of it all
the magic and mystery
the journey, be it big or small
living the outstanding victory
transformation so raw
dreaming of guided synchronicity
their hearts beat in awe
reaching a soul's light
is not of simplicity.

Till our last day, our last moment, our last breath,
we will be transforming. We will always be running
through the cycles.

We are all main characters.
Overlapped in thousands of stories
and millions of moments.

## MONARCH

For it's all but a memory
small pockets of time
etched in the photos
or the backs of our minds.

*Monarch*

Weightless
flying free I am
I share my colors
no longer a meek little lamb.

Soaring
my wings can't be touched
higher off the ground
but finally, *I'm safe and sound.*

To my fellow Monarchs,

Thank you for coming along on this journey with me and giving my words a beautiful home. Now that it's time to go back into the world, remember— the path less traveled can be remarkable. With each step along the way, share your kindness and be brave.

I send you with serenity.

*Alex*

www.ingramcontent.com/pod-product-compliance
Lightning Source LLC
LaVergne TN
LVHW051040070526
838201LV00067B/4880